CARSTEN GERLITZ

THE CELTIC CHOIRBOOK

meinen Eltern

GREENLAND MUSIC

SCHOTT

Carsten Gerlitz, a native of Berlin, studied music and information technology. He is an accomplished musician, choral conductor, composer-arranger, and author for a number of publishers and labels. In addition, Carsten owns and operates a fully equipped recording studio where he produces musical, as well as narrative works for a wide variety of professional clients. His a cappella choir, THE HAPPY DISHARMONISTS, have performed, toured, and recorded for many years, and the numerous CD's and being awarded the coveted Berlin Culture Prize attest to Carsten's creative talents!

Carsten Gerlitz, geboren in Berlin, studierte Musik und Informatik und arbeitet als Musiker, Chorleiter, Arrangeur und Autor für verschiedene Verlage und Labels. Im eigenen Tonstudio betreut und leitet er Wort- und Musikproduktionen. Mit seinem Chor THE HAPPY DISHARMONISTS produzierte er verschiedene CDs und erhielt den Berliner Kulturpreis „BONZO".

www.greenlandmusic.de

CELTIC CHOIRBOOK
© 2004 by Greenlandmusic, Berlin
im Vertrieb von Schott Musik International
Bestellnummer Schott: ED 9760
ISMN M-001-13706-5
www.schott-music.com
Cover: Carsten Gerlitz, Berlin
Lektorat: Irene Wohlfahrt, Berlin & Gunter Berger, Leipzig
Textübersetzung: Hans Matschukat, Walla Walla (Washington, USA)
Notensatz: Johannes Rauterberg, Leipzig

Inhalt

Londonderry Air

Traditional
Arr.: Carsten Gerlitz

5

6

7

Auld Lang Syne

Traditional
Arr.: Carsten Gerlitz

Amazing Grace

Traditional
Arr.: Carsten Gerlitz

12

13

EARLY ONE MORNING

Traditional
Arr.: Carsten Gerlitz

15

Lullaby

Traditional
Arr.: Carsten Gerlitz

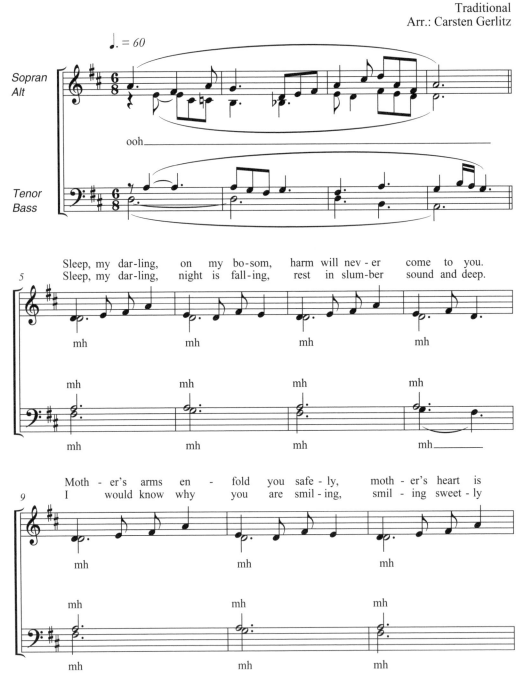

Sleep, my dar-ling, on my bo-som, harm will nev-er come to you.
Sleep, my dar-ling, night is fall-ing, rest in slum-ber sound and deep.

Moth-er's arms en-fold you safe-ly, moth-er's heart is
I would know why you are smil-ing, smil-ing sweet-ly

3. Don't be frightened, it's a leaflet
Tapping, tapping on the door;
Don't be frightened, 'twas a wavelet,
Sighing, sighing on the shore.
Slumber, slumber, nought can hurt you,
Nothing bring you harm or fright.
Slumber, darling, smiling sweetly
At those angels robed in white.

19

Dacw 'Nghariad i Lawr yn y Berllan
(Look! There Is My Love)

Traditional
Arr.: Carsten Gerlitz

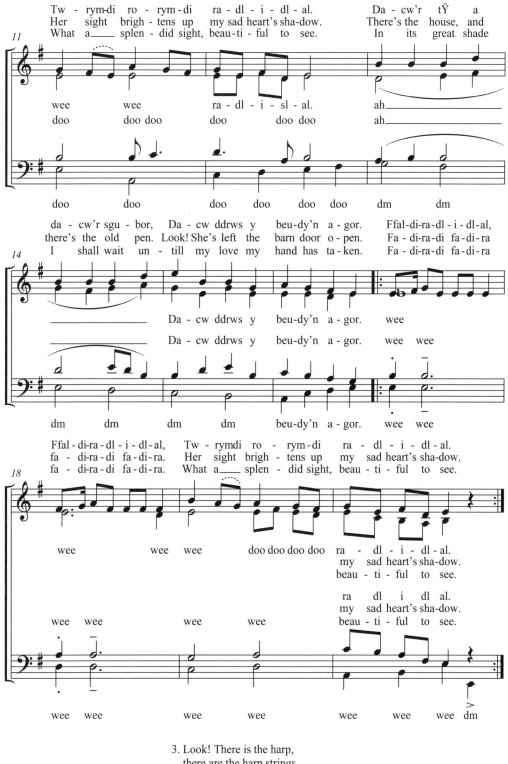

3. Look! There is the harp,
   there are the harp strings.
   No one to play them now -
   just useless old things.
   Look! There is the dainty maiden
   with her song my heart has taken.

CARRICKFERGUS

Traditional
Arr.: Carsten Gerlitz

© *2004 by GREENLANDMUSIC BERLIN*

2. and hand-some ro - ver ___ from town to town

and hand-some ro - ver ___ from town to town

and hand-some ooh ___

and hand-some ooh doo doo doo doo doo

Ah but I'm sick now, ___ my days are num-ber-ed

Ah but I'm sick now, ___ ooh ___

Ah but I'm ooh ___ doo doo

doo doo doo doo doo doo doo

come all ___ you young men ___ and lay me down.

come all ___ you young men ___ and lay me down.

doo come all ___ you young men ___ and lay me down.

doo doo doo doo doo

25

SALLY GARDENS

Traditional
Arr.: Carsten Gerlitz

3. Down by the Sally gardens, my love and I did meet,
   she passed the Sally gardens, with little snow-white feet,
   she bid me „Take love easy, as the leaves grow on the tree."
   But I being young and foolish, with her did not agree.

WILL YE GO, LASSIE, GO?

Traditional
Arr.: Carsten Gerlitz

2. I will build my love a tower near yon pure crystal fountain
   and on it I will pile all the flowers of the mountain,
   will ye go, lassie, go?

3. If my true love she were gone, I would surely find another,
   where wild mountain thyme grows around the blooming heather
   will ye go, lassie, go?

Whiskey In The Jar

Traditional
Arr.: Carsten Gerlitz

2. I counted out his money
   and it made a pretty penny,
   I put it in my pocket
   to take home to darlin' Jenny,
   She sighed and swore she loved me
   and never would decieve me,
   But the devil take the women,
   for they always lie so easy.
   Musha ...

3. I went into me chamber
   all for to take a slumber,
   To dream of gold and girls
   and of course it was no wonder.
   Me Jenny took me charges,
   and she filled them up with water,
   Called on Captain Farrell
   to get ready for the slaughter.
   Musha ...

An Irish Blessing

Traditional
Arr.: Carsten Gerlitz

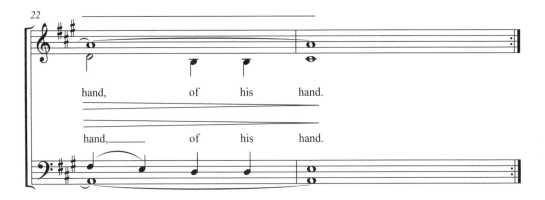

RIVERDANCE

Carsten Gerlitz

35

All Through The Night

(Ar Hyd Y Nos)

Traditional
Arr.: Carsten Gerlitz

© 2004 by GREENLANDMUSIC BERLIN

39

GIN A BODY

COMIN' THRO' THE RYE

Traditional
Arr.: Carsten Gerlitz

41

Believe Me, If All Those Endearing Young Charms

Traditional
Arr.: Carsten Gerlitz

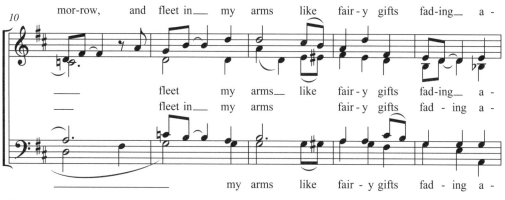

SCARBOROUGH FAIR

Traditional
Arr.: Carsten Gerlitz

45

3. Tell her to wash it yonder dry well,
   parsley, sage, Rosemary and thyme.
   Where water ne'er sprung, nor drop of rain fell,
   and then she'll be a true love of mine.

4. Tell her to dry it yonder thorn,
   parsley, sage, Rosemary and thyme.
   Which never bore blossom since Adam was born,
   and then she'll be a true love of mine.

GREENSLEEVES

Traditional
Arr.: Carsten Gerlitz

3. Alas, my love, that you should own
   A heart of wanton vanity,
   So must I meditate alone
   Upon your insincerity.

4. Ah, Greensleeves, now farewell, adieu,
   To God I pray to prosper thee,
   For I am still your lover true,
   Come once again and love me!

THE FIRST NOEL

Traditional
Arr.: Carsten Gerlitz

10

cer - tain poor shep-herds in fields as they lay. In___ fields___ where they
in_____ the east_____ be - yond___ them far; and to_____ the___

cer - tain poor shep-herds in fields they lay.___ In fields___ where they
in_____ the east_____ be - yond them far;___ and to_____ the___

cer-tain poor shep-herds fields lay fields
in__ the east___ far, far, to

poor shep - herds fields lay fields they
east be - yond far, far, to___ the

15

lay a - keep-ing their sheep on a cold win-ter's night__ that
earth it__ gave__ great light, and so it con - ti - nued both

lay___ keep sheep on a cold win-ter's night__
earth__ great light and so it con - ti - nued

lay___ no - el no - el on a cold night
earth__ no - el no - el so con - ti - - - nued

lay no - - - el cold night___ that
earth no - - - el great light___ both

51

was___ so deep. *f* No - el,___ No - el, No - el, No -
day___ and night.

was so deep. *f* No - el,___ No - el, No - el, No -
day and night.

was___ so deep. *f* No - el, No - el,___ No - el,___ No -
day___ and night.

was deep. *f* No - el, No - el, No, - no -
day night.

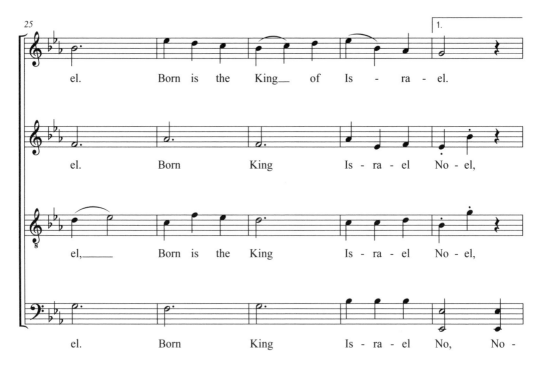

el. Born is the King___ of Is - ra - el.

el. Born King Is - ra - el No - el,

el,___ Born is the King Is - ra - el No - el,

el. Born King Is - ra - el No, No -

52

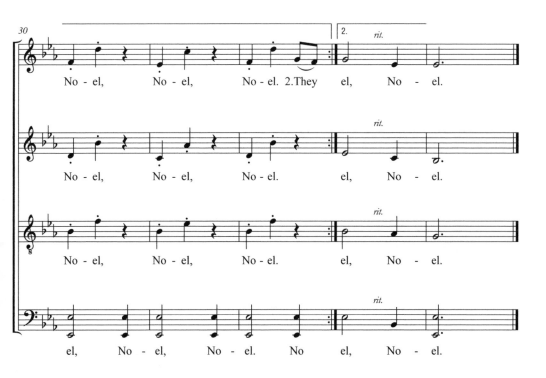

30

No - el,   No - el,   No - el. 2.They   el,   No - el.

No - el,   No - el,   No - el.   el,   No - el.

No - el,   No - el,   No - el.   el,   No - el.

el,   No - el,   No - el.   No   el,   No - el.

3. This star drew nigh to the northwest,
   o'er Bethlehem it took its rest,
   and there it did both stop and stay,
   right over the place where Jesus lay.
   Noel, Noel, Noel, Noel,
   born is the King of Israel.

4. Then let us all with one accord
   sing praises to our heavenly Lord,
   that hath made heaven and earth of nought,
   and with his blood mankind hath bought.
   Noel, Noel, Noel, Noel,
   born is the King of Israel.

Botany Bay

Traditional
Arr.: Carsten Gerlitz

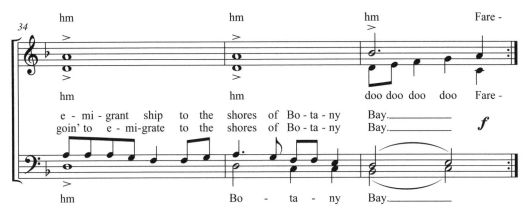

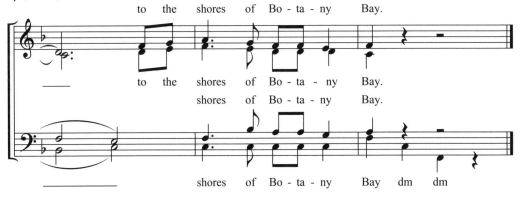

3. And when I reach Australia
   I'll go and look for gold
   sure there's plenty there for the digging
   or so I have been told
   or I might go back into my trade
   eight hundred bricks I'll lay
   in an eight hour day for eight bob pay
   on the shores of Botany Bay.

THE WILD ROVER

Traditional
Arr.: Carsten Gerlitz

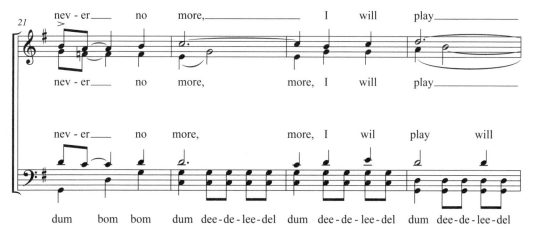

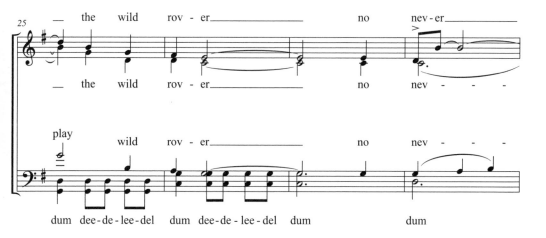

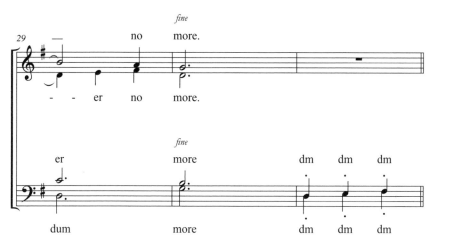

Da capo al fine